delicious diabetic recipes

Simply Sensational Desserts

simply sensational dessserts

Raspberry Napoleons

1¼ **cups low-fat (1%) milk**
  1 **package (4-serving size) vanilla fat-free sugar-free instant**
    pudding and pie filling mix
  1 **tablespoon amaretto liqueur** *or* ¼ **teaspoon almond**
    extract
  6 **sheets frozen phyllo dough, thawed**
  2 **cups fresh raspberries**
  2 **teaspoons powdered sugar**

1. Preheat oven to 350°F. Whisk milk and pudding mix in medium bowl 2 minutes. Stir in amaretto; cover and refrigerate.

2. Working quickly, place 1 phyllo sheet on large work surface; coat lightly with nonstick cooking spray. Top with 2 more phyllo sheets, spraying each with cooking spray. Cut stacked dough crosswise into 6 strips. Cut each strip in half to form 12 rectangles. Transfer rectangles to ungreased baking sheet. Repeat process with remaining 3 phyllo sheets; place on second baking sheet. Bake 6 to 8 minutes or until golden brown and crisp. Remove to wire racks to cool completely.

3. To assemble, spread half of pudding over 8 rectangles; top with half of raspberries. Repeat layers with 8 phyllo rectangles, remaining pudding and raspberries; top with remaining 8 phyllo rectangles. Sprinkle with powdered sugar before serving.

Makes 8 servings

Nutrients per Serving: 1 napoleon
Calories: 130, **Calories from Fat:** 12%, **Total Fat:** 2g,
Saturated Fat: 1g, **Cholesterol:** 3mg, **Sodium:** 253mg,
Carbohydrate: 25g, **Fiber:** 2g, **Protein:** 3g

Dietary Exchanges: ½ Fruit, 1 Starch, ½ Fat

Lemon Poppy Seed Bundt Cake

1 cup granulated sugar
½ cup (1 stick) butter, softened
1 egg, at room temperature
2 egg whites, at room temperature
¾ cup low-fat (1%) milk
2 teaspoons vanilla
2 cups all-purpose flour
2 tablespoons poppy seeds
1 tablespoon grated lemon peel
2 teaspoons baking powder
¼ teaspoon salt
4½ teaspoons powdered sugar

1. Preheat oven to 350°F. Grease and flour 10-inch bundt pan.

2. Beat granulated sugar, butter, egg and egg whites in large bowl with electric mixer at medium speed until well blended. Add milk and vanilla; mix well. Add flour, poppy seeds, lemon peel, baking powder and salt; beat about 2 minutes or until smooth. Pour batter into prepared pan.

3. Bake 30 minutes or until toothpick inserted near center comes out clean. Gently loosen cake from pan with knife; turn out onto wire rack. Cool completely. Sprinkle with powdered sugar. Cut into 16 pieces. *Makes 16 servings*

Tip: Freshly grated lemon peel provides a flavor that dried lemon peel cannot match. One medium lemon equals approximately 1 tablespoon of grated lemon peel. When grating lemon peel, avoid the bitter white layer known as the pith.

Nutrients per Serving: 1 slice cake (¹⁄₁₆ of total recipe)
Calories: 178, **Calories from Fat:** 35%, **Total Fat:** 7g,
Saturated Fat: 1g, **Cholesterol:** 14mg, **Sodium:** 181mg,
Carbohydrate: 26g, **Fiber:** 1g, **Protein:** 3g

Dietary Exchanges: 2 Starch, 1 Fat

Enlightened Banana Upside-Down Cake

½ **cup sugar**
1 **tablespoon water**
2 **tablespoons butter**
2 **small bananas, cut into ¼-inch slices**
1½ **cups all-purpose flour**
2 **teaspoons baking powder**
½ **teaspoon salt**
¾ **cup sugar substitute***
¼ **cup canola oil**
¼ **cup unsweetened applesauce**
2 **egg whites**
1 **egg**
½ **cup low-fat buttermilk**
1 **teaspoon vanilla**

This recipe was tested with sucralose-based sugar substitute.

1. Preheat oven to 325°F.

2. Combine sugar and water in small saucepan. Heat over medium-high heat, stirring constantly, until mixture is amber in color. Stir in butter. Immediately pour into 8-inch square nonstick baking pan. Arrange banana slices in sugar mixture.

3. Sift flour, baking powder and salt into medium bowl. Beat sugar substitute, oil and applesauce in large bowl with electric mixer at medium speed 1 minute. Beat in egg whites and egg, 1 at a time, until blended. Beat in buttermilk and vanilla. Gradually add flour mixture; beat 1 minute or until blended. Pour batter over bananas in pan.

4. Bake 30 to 35 minutes or until toothpick inserted into center comes out clean. Cool 5 minutes in pan on wire rack. Invert onto serving plate. Cool slightly; cut into 12 pieces. Serve warm or at room temperature.   *Makes 12 servings*

Nutrients per Serving: 1 slice cake (¹⁄₁₂ of total recipe)
Calories: 184, **Calories from Fat:** 35%, **Total Fat:** 7g,
Saturated Fat: 2g, **Cholesterol:** 23mg, **Sodium:** 191mg,
Carbohydrate: 27g, **Fiber:** 1g, **Protein:** 3g

Dietary Exchanges: ½ Fruit, 1½ Starch, 1 Fat

Berry-Peachy Cobbler

4 tablespoons plus 2 teaspoons sugar, divided
¾ cup plus 2 tablespoons all-purpose flour, divided
1¼ pounds peaches, peeled and sliced *or* 1 package
    (16 ounces) frozen unsweetened sliced peaches,
    thawed and drained
2 cups fresh raspberries *or* 1 package (12 ounces) frozen
    unsweetened raspberries
1 teaspoon grated lemon peel
½ teaspoon baking powder
½ teaspoon baking soda
⅛ teaspoon salt
2 tablespoons cold margarine, cut into small pieces
½ cup low-fat buttermilk

1. Preheat oven to 425°F. Spray 8 custard cups or 11×7-inch baking dish with nonstick cooking spray; place custard cups on jelly-roll pan.

2. Combine 2 tablespoons sugar and 2 tablespoons flour in large bowl. Add peaches, raspberries and lemon peel; toss to coat. Divide fruit evenly among prepared custard cups. Bake about 15 minutes or until fruit is bubbly around edges.

3. Meanwhile, combine remaining ¾ cup flour, 2 tablespoons sugar, baking powder, baking soda and salt in medium bowl. Cut in margarine with pastry blender or 2 knives until mixture resembles coarse crumbs. Stir in buttermilk just until dry ingredients are moistened.

4. Remove custard cups from oven; top fruit with equal dollops of topping. Sprinkle topping with remaining 2 teaspoons sugar. Bake 18 to 20 minutes or until topping is lightly browned. Serve warm. *Makes 8 servings*

Nutrients per Serving: 1 dessert (⅛ of total recipe)
Calories: 149, **Calories from Fat:** 20%, **Total Fat:** 3g,
Saturated Fat: 1g, **Cholesterol:** 1mg, **Sodium:** 195mg,
Carbohydrate: 28g, **Fiber:** 3g, **Protein:** 3g

Dietary Exchanges: 1 Fruit, 1 Starch, ½ Fat

Oatmeal-Date Cookies

½ cup packed light brown sugar
¼ cup (½ stick) margarine, softened
1 egg
1 egg white
1 tablespoon thawed frozen apple juice concentrate
1 teaspoon vanilla
1½ cups all-purpose flour
2 teaspoons baking soda
¼ teaspoon salt
1½ cups quick oats
½ cup chopped dates or raisins

1. Preheat oven to 350°F. Lightly spray cookie sheets with nonstick cooking spray.

2. Beat brown sugar and margarine in large bowl until well blended. Add egg, egg white, apple juice concentrate and vanilla; mix well.

3. Add flour, baking soda and salt; mix well. Stir in oats and dates. Drop dough by teaspoonfuls onto prepared cookie sheets.

4. Bake 8 to 10 minutes or until edges are very lightly browned. (Centers should still be soft.) Cool 1 minute on cookie sheets. Remove to wire racks; cool completely.

Makes 3 dozen cookies

Nutrients per Serving: 1 cookie
Calories: 65, **Calories from Fat:** 27%, **Total Fat:** 2g,
Saturated Fat: <1g, **Cholesterol:** 6mg, **Sodium:** 106mg,
Carbohydrate: 11g, **Fiber:** 1g, **Protein:** 1g

Dietary Exchanges: 1 Starch

Lemon-Cranberry Bars

½ cup sugar substitute
½ cup thawed frozen lemonade concentrate
¼ cup (½ stick) margarine, softened
1 egg
1½ cups all-purpose flour
2 teaspoons grated lemon peel
½ teaspoon baking soda
½ teaspoon salt
½ cup dried cranberries

1. Preheat oven to 375°F. Lightly spray 8-inch square baking pan with nonstick cooking spray.

2. Combine sugar substitute, lemonade concentrate, margarine and egg in medium bowl; mix well. Add flour, lemon peel, baking soda and salt; mix well. Stir in cranberries; spoon batter into prepared pan.

3. Bake 20 minutes or until golden brown. Cool completely in pan on wire rack. Cut into 16 bars.   *Makes 16 bars*

Nutrients per Serving: 1 bar (¹⁄₁₆ of total recipe)
Calories: 104, **Calories from Fat:** 26%, **Total Fat:** 3g,
Saturated Fat: 1g, **Cholesterol:** 13mg, **Sodium:** 150mg,
Carbohydrate: 15g, **Fiber:** <1g, **Protein:** 3g

Dietary Exchanges: 1 Starch, ½ Fat

Hidden Pumpkin Pies

1½ **cups solid-pack pumpkin**
  1 **cup evaporated skimmed milk**
  ½ **cup cholesterol-free egg substitute** *or* 2 **eggs**
  ¼ **cup sugar substitute***
1¼ **teaspoons vanilla, divided**
  1 **teaspoon pumpkin pie spice****
  3 **egg whites**
  ¼ **teaspoon cream of tartar**
  ⅓ **cup honey**

*This recipe was tested with sucralose-based sugar substitute.

**Substitute ½ teaspoon ground cinnamon, ¼ teaspoon ground ginger and ⅛ teaspoon each ground allspice and ground nutmeg for 1 teaspoon pumpkin pie spice, if desired.

1. Preheat oven to 350°F.

2. Combine pumpkin, evaporated milk, egg substitute, sugar substitute, 1 teaspoon vanilla and pumpkin pie spice in large bowl; mix well. Pour into 6 (6-ounce) custard cups or soufflé dishes. Place in shallow baking dish or pan. Pour boiling water around custard cups to depth of 1 inch. Bake 25 minutes or until set.

3. Meanwhile, beat egg whites, cream of tartar and remaining ¼ teaspoon vanilla in medium bowl with electric mixer at high speed until soft peaks form. Gradually add honey, beating until stiff peaks form.

4. Spread egg white mixture over tops of hot pumpkin pies. Return to oven; bake 8 to 12 minutes or until tops of pies are golden brown. Let stand 10 minutes. Serve warm.

Makes 6 servings

Nutrients per Serving: 1 pie (⅙ of total recipe)
Calories: 148, **Calories from Fat:** 10%, **Total Fat:** 2g,
Saturated Fat: 1g, **Cholesterol:** 54mg, **Sodium:** 133mg,
Carbohydrate: 27g, **Fiber:** 2g, **Protein:** 8g

Dietary Exchanges: 2 Starch

Chocolate Pudding Cake Squares

CAKE
- 1 cup all-purpose flour
- ½ cup warm fat-free (skim) milk
- ⅓ cup granulated sugar
- 10 packets sugar substitute *or* equivalent of 20 teaspoons sugar
- 3 tablespoons unsweetened cocoa powder
- 2 tablespoons canola oil
- 2 teaspoons baking powder
- 2 teaspoons vanilla
- ½ teaspoon salt

SAUCE
- ¼ cup sugar
- 10 packets sugar substitute *or* equivalent of 20 teaspoons sugar
- 3 tablespoons unsweetened cocoa powder
- 1¾ cups boiling water

1. Preheat oven to 350°F. For cake, beat flour, milk, ⅓ cup sugar, 10 packets sugar substitute, 3 tablespoons cocoa, oil, baking powder, vanilla and salt in large bowl; beat with electric mixer at medium speed 2 minutes or until well blended. Pour into ungreased 9-inch square baking pan.

2. For sauce, sprinkle ¼ cup sugar, 10 packets sugar substitute and 3 tablespoons cocoa over batter in pan. Pour boiling water over top. *Do not stir.*

3. Bake 40 minutes or until cake portion has risen to top of pan and sauce is bubbly underneath. Cool 10 minutes. Cut into 9 squares. Serve warm.   *Makes 9 servings*

Nutrients per Serving: 1 square (⅑ of total recipe)
Calories: 150, **Calories from Fat:** 18%, **Total Fat:** 3g,
Saturated Fat: <1g, **Cholesterol:** <1mg, **Sodium:** 246mg,
Carbohydrate: 26g, **Fiber:** <1g, **Protein:** 4g

Dietary Exchanges: 2 Starch, ½ Fat

Farmhouse Lemon Meringue Pie

1 frozen pie crust
4 eggs, at room temperature
3 tablespoons lemon juice
2 tablespoons reduced-fat margarine, melted
2 teaspoons grated lemon peel
3 drops yellow food coloring (optional)
1 cup cold water
½ cup sugar, divided
3 tablespoons cornstarch
3 packets sugar substitute*
⅛ teaspoon salt
¼ teaspoon vanilla

This recipe was tested with sucralose-based sugar substitute.

1. Preheat oven to 425°F. Bake pie crust according to package directions.

2. Separate eggs; discard 2 egg yolks. Mix lemon juice, margarine, lemon peel and food coloring in small bowl.

3. Combine water, 6 tablespoons sugar, cornstarch, sugar substitute and salt in medium saucepan; whisk until smooth. Heat over medium-high heat, whisking until mixture begins to boil. Reduce heat to medium. Boil 1 minute, stirring constantly; remove from heat. Stir ¼ cup sugar mixture into egg yolks; whisk until blended. Slowly whisk egg yolk mixture back into sugar mixture. Cook over medium heat 3 minutes, whisking constantly. Remove from heat; stir in lemon juice mixture until blended. Pour into baked pie crust.

4. Beat egg whites in large bowl with electric mixer at high speed until soft peaks form. Gradually beat in remaining 2 tablespoons sugar and vanilla; beat until stiff peaks form. Spread meringue over pie filling with rubber spatula, making sure it completely covers filling and touches edge of pie crust. Bake 5 to 10 minutes or until lightly browned. Cool completely on wire rack. Refrigerate 8 hours or overnight.

Makes 8 servings

Nutrients per Serving: 1 slice pie (⅛ of total recipe)
Calories: 170, **Calories from Fat:** 42%, **Total Fat:** 8g,
Saturated Fat: 2g, **Cholesterol:** 54mg, **Sodium:** 166mg,
Carbohydrate: 25g, **Fiber:** <1g, **Protein:** 4g

Dietary Exchanges: 2 Starch, 2 Fat

Chocolate Bundt Cake with White Chocolate Glaze

CAKE
- 1 package (about 18 ounces) chocolate cake mix
- ¾ cup cholesterol-free egg substitute *or* 3 eggs
- 3 jars (2½ ounces each) puréed baby food prunes
- ¾ cup warm water
- 2 tablespoons canola oil
- 2 to 3 teaspoons instant coffee granules

GLAZE (optional)
- ½ cup white chocolate chips
- 1 tablespoon milk

1. Preheat oven to 350°F. Lightly grease and flour 12-cup bundt pan.

2. For cake, beat cake mix, egg substitute, prunes, water, oil and coffee granules in large bowl with electric mixer at high speed 2 minutes. Pour into prepared pan. Bake 40 minutes or until toothpick inserted near center comes out clean. Cool in pan on wire rack 10 minutes. Invert cake onto serving plate; cool completely.

3. For glaze, combine white chocolate chips and milk in small microwavable bowl. Microwave on MEDIUM (50%) 50 seconds; stir. Microwave on MEDIUM (50%) at additional 30-second intervals until chips are completely melted; stir after each 30-second interval.

4. Pour warm glaze over cooled cake. Let stand about 30 minutes before serving.   *Makes 16 servings*

Nutrients per Serving: 1 slice cake (1/16 of total recipe)
Calories: 177, **Calories from Fat:** 36%, **Total Fat:** 7g,
Saturated Fat: 1g, **Cholesterol:** <1mg, **Sodium:** 292mg,
Carbohydrate: 27g, **Fiber:** 1g, **Protein:** 4g

Dietary Exchanges: 2 Starch, 2 Fat

Mocha Cappuccino Ice Cream Pie

¼ cup cold water
1 tablespoon instant coffee granules
4 packets sugar substitute *or* **equivalent of 8 teaspoons**
  sugar
½ teaspoon vanilla
4 cups fat-free sugar-free fudge marble ice cream,
  slightly softened
1 vanilla wafer pie crust

1. Combine water, coffee granules, sugar substitute and vanilla in small bowl; stir until granules dissolve.

2. Combine ice cream and coffee mixture in large bowl; stir gently until liquid is blended into ice cream. Spoon into pie crust; smooth top with rubber spatula.

3. Cover with plastic wrap; freeze about 4 hours or until firm. Cut into 8 slices. *Makes 8 servings*

Variation: Omit pie crust and serve filling in dessert cups with biscotti.

Nutrients per Serving: 1 slice pie (⅛ of total recipe)
Calories: 201, **Calories from Fat:** 34%, **Total Fat:** 8g,
Saturated Fat: 2g, **Cholesterol:** 9mg, **Sodium:** 159mg,
Carbohydrate: 29g, **Fiber:** 0g, **Protein:** 5g

Dietary Exchanges: 2 Starch, 1½ Fat

Caribbean Cake Squares

- 1 package (9 ounces) yellow cake mix
- ½ cup orange juice
- 2 egg whites
- 2 cans (8 ounces each) crushed pineapple in juice
  Additional orange juice
- 1 tablespoon cornstarch
- ½ cup slivered almonds
- ½ cup unsweetened shredded coconut
- 2 large ripe bananas
- 1 can (15 ounces) mandarin orange segments in light syrup, drained

1. Preheat oven to 350°F. Spray 13×9-inch nonstick baking pan with nonstick cooking spray.

2. Beat cake mix, ½ cup orange juice and egg whites in medium bowl with electric mixer at medium speed 2 minutes or until well blended. Spoon batter evenly into prepared pan.

3. Bake 11 to 12 minutes or until toothpick inserted into center comes out clean. Cool completely in pan on wire rack.

4. Drain juice from pineapple into 2-cup measure; reserve crushed pineapple. Add additional orange juice to measure 1½ cups liquid. Stir in cornstarch until smooth. Bring juice mixture to a boil in medium saucepan over high heat, stirring constantly. Boil 1 minute, stirring constantly. Remove from heat.

5. Heat almonds and coconut in large skillet over medium heat until golden brown, stirring frequently.

6. Spread pineapple evenly over cake. Slice bananas and arrange over pineapple. Top with mandarin orange segments. Carefully drizzle juice mixture evenly over topping. Sprinkle with almond mixture. Cover and refrigerate 1 to 4 hours. Cut into 16 squares. *Makes 16 servings*

Nutrients per Serving: 1 square (¹⁄₁₆ of total recipe)
Calories: 148, **Calories from Fat:** 29%, **Total Fat:** 5g,
Saturated Fat: 1g, **Cholesterol:** <1mg, **Sodium:** 115mg,
Carbohydrate: 25g, **Fiber:** 2g, **Protein:** 2g

Dietary Exchanges: 2 Starch, 1 Fat

Lemon Mousse Squares

1 cup graham cracker crumbs
2 tablespoons reduced-fat margarine, melted
1 packet sugar substitute *or* equivalent of 2 teaspoons
      sugar
⅓ cup cold water
1 envelope (¼ ounce) unflavored gelatin
2 eggs, well beaten
2 teaspoons grated lemon peel
½ cup lemon juice
¼ cup sugar
2 cups fat-free whipped topping
1 container (6 ounces) lemon fat-free sugar-free yogurt

1. Spray 9-inch square baking pan with nonstick cooking spray. Combine graham cracker crumbs, margarine and sugar substitute in small bowl. Press onto bottom of prepared pan.

2. Combine cold water and gelatin in small microwavable bowl; let stand 2 minutes. Microwave on HIGH 40 seconds to dissolve gelatin.

3. Combine eggs, lemon peel, lemon juice and sugar in top of double boiler. Cook over boiling water, stirring constantly, about 4 minutes or until thickened. Remove from heat; stir in gelatin mixture. Refrigerate about 25 minutes or until mixture is thoroughly cooled and begins to set.

4. Gently whisk lemon-gelatin mixture, whipped topping and yogurt just until combined. Pour into prepared crust. Refrigerate 1 hour or until firm. Cut into 9 squares.   *Makes 9 servings*

Nutrients per Serving: 1 square (⅑ of total recipe)
Calories: 154, **Calories from Fat:** 29%, **Total Fat:** 5g,
Saturated Fat: 1g, **Cholesterol:** 47mg, **Sodium:** 124mg,
Carbohydrate: 24g, **Fiber:** 1g, **Protein:** 3g

Dietary Exchanges: 1½ Starch, 1 Fat

Cranberry Phyllo Cheesecake Tarts

1 cup fresh or frozen cranberries
¼ cup sugar
1 teaspoon grated orange peel
2 tablespoons orange juice
¼ teaspoon ground allspice
6 sheets phyllo dough (14×9-inch sheets), thawed
1 container (8 ounces) reduced-fat whipped cream cheese
8 ounces vanilla fat-free yogurt
1 tablespoon sugar or sugar substitute, divided
1 teaspoon vanilla

1. Preheat oven to 350°F. Combine cranberries, ¼ cup sugar, orange peel, orange juice and allspice in small saucepan. Cook and stir over medium heat until berries pop and mixture thickens. Set aside to cool completely.

2. Lightly spray 12 standard (2½-inch) muffin cups with butter-flavored cooking spray. Cut phyllo sheets in half lengthwise, then crosswise into thirds. Spray 1 phyllo square lightly with cooking spray. Top with second square, slightly offsetting corners; spray lightly with cooking spray. Top with third square. Place stack of phyllo squares into 1 prepared muffin cup, pressing into bottom and up side of cup. Repeat with remaining phyllo squares. Bake 3 to 4 minutes or until golden. Cool completely in pan on wire rack.

3. Beat cream cheese, yogurt, 1 tablespoon sugar and vanilla in medium bowl with electric mixer until smooth. Divide mixture evenly among phyllo cups. Top evenly with cranberry mixture.

Makes 12 servings

Nutrients per Serving: 1 tart (¹⁄₁₂ of total recipe)
Calories: 104, **Calories from Fat:** 34%, **Total Fat:** 4g,
Saturated Fat: 2g, **Cholesterol:** 11mg, **Sodium:** 113mg,
Carbohydrate: 14g, **Fiber:** 5g, **Protein:** 3g

Dietary Exchanges: 1 Starch, ½ Fat